Edward Monson George

The Silver and Indian Currency Questions Treated in a

Practical Manner

Edward Monson George

The Silver and Indian Currency Questions Treated in a Practical Manner

ISBN/EAN: 9783337304119

Printed in Europe, USA, Canada, Australia, Japan

Cover: Foto ©ninafisch / pixelio.de

More available books at **www.hansebooks.com**

THE SILVER AND
INDIAN CURRENCY QUESTIONS

TREATED IN

A PRACTICAL MANNER

BY

E. MONSON GEORGE. M.Inst.C.E.

London:

EFFINGHAM WILSON & CO.,

ROYAL EXCHANGE.

MDCCCXCIV.

CONTENTS.

INTRODUCTION.

In the following pages it has been endeavoured to call attention to the great evil to the universe, and India and Great Britain in particular, caused by the depreciation in the gold value of silver, or what is the same thing, the appreciation in the silver value of gold. The author has tried his best to put the matter in as clear and simple a manner as possible, and in few words, so that all who read them can at once understand and grasp the question.

CHAPTER I. deals with the question of closing the Indian mints to the free coinage of silver, and points out the effect of this action on the trade of India and England.

CHAPTER II. shows what might have been the result on the finances of India if the mints had not been closed, and describes how the fall in the gold value of silver affects the price of produce in England.

CHAPTER III. explains what would be the result as regards the sale of Secretary of States drafts in London if a minimum rate was fixed above the current rate of exchange. On this question there have been widely divergent views, especially in India.

CHAPTER IV. points out the relation between the export and import trade of India and the currency question, and the consequent danger to trade by closing the Indian mints.

CHAPTER V. discusses the subject of an introduction of a gold standard into India. This matter has been the subject of much argument for many years both in England and India. It has been thought by many who have not carefully studied the question that, provided the natives of India did not absorb the gold introduced for purposes of hoarding, no other special difficulty in the introduction of a gold standard could arise. This fallacy has been exposed in this chapter.

CHAPTER VI. deals with the silver problem generally. It shows how the question has in a great measure arisen through the action of England herself. It shows further the terrible depression in trade the depreciation in the gold value of silver has caused in Europe and its danger to illicit coinage. It discusses the proposal of the introduction of " International Bimetallism," and finally points out a more easy method of settling the question.

CHAPTER VII. points out the difficulties of the situation with the Indian mints closed, and gives reasons for not re-opening the mints until some settlement has been come to with other nations as to the protection of the precious metals used for currency purposes.

The Author hopes that this little book may prove acceptable to the general public, and help to elucidate a question that is much occupying attention at the present time.

THE SILVER AND
INDIAN CURRENCY QUESTIONS
Treated in a Practical Manner.

CHAPTER I.

RESULT ON ENGLAND AND INDIA CAUSED BY CLOSING THE INDIAN MINTS TO FREE COINAGE.

FOR many years there have been advocates in India for closing the Indian mints to the free coinage of rupees. As early as 1876 the Government of India were approached on this question, and it was then thought best not to do anything to support the gold value of the rupee. Since the year 1876 the exchange value of the rupee has fallen from 18½d., the lowest point touched in that year, to 14½d. in the early part of 1893, the price of silver at that time being 37d. an ounce. There appeared every reason to expect a further considerable fall in the price of silver owing principally to the probable repeal of the Sherman Act in the United States of America.

It therefore seemed absolutely necessary to take some action to protect the silver currency of India. After many months' delay, and after receiving the report of the Herschell Commission, the Government of India, with the concurrence of the Secretary of State for India, finally decided to close the Indian mints to the free coinage of silver. A law to this effect was passed in June, 1893, and exchange, which at that time was about 14¾d., at once rebounded to 16d. The Government of India at the same time also offered to receive sovereigns into the Treasuries at the rate of 15 rupees to a sovereign, this rate being equivalent to an exchange of 16d.

There were many in India who looked upon the currency question as regards India as practically settled ; the Council Bills sold in London the same week as the announcement of the closing of the Indian mints was published, at about 16d., as compared to a much lower rate in previous weeks.

On the other hand silver, which at the time of the closing of the mints was about 37d., rapidly fell to 30d. an ounce.

A very short time was, however, necessary to show that the closing of the Indian mints had by no means cured the evil from which India had been suffering for twenty years.

The Council Bills, which it was thought generally in India would now only be sold in London at 16d., were still allotted at rates below this figure. Owing partly to an outcry in India, an effort was made to adhere to a minimum of 1s. 3¼d. in allotting Council Bills.

In consequence of this action, the bills could not be sold, and for many weeks no allotments were made. The Secretary of State for India, in order to meet India's gold obligations in England, was therefore compelled to raise several millions sterling in the London market. In the meantime rupees were accumulating in the reserve Treasuries of India, and on the 22nd March, 1894, they amounted to 26 crores.

Early in 1894 the Government of India decided on a new departure. Exchange had up to that date kept pretty steady for some time at 15d., but the Council Bills had only been taken up in small quantities.

The Secretary of State for India therefore

determined to sell the Council Bills at the market rate, and not to adhere to any fixed minimum. In consequence of this action large quantities of Bills were sold, but exchange fell to 13½d.

Having now given a short account of the action of the Indian Government in closing the Indian mints, the effect of this action on England and India will be considered.

It will be shown in Chapter II. how and why the produce of a country with a silver currency always remains the same in value, notwithstanding any variation in the gold price of silver. The same chapter will also show why the price of produce in a country with a gold standard falls and rises with the gold price of silver.

The Indian Government, by closing the Indian mints, and refusing to allow merchants and others to send bar silver to the mints for conversion into rupees, have forced up the gold value of the rupee from 10¼d., its natural price with silver at 27d. an ounce, to about 14d., the rate of exchange in March, 1894.

In other silver currency countries, such as China, Mexico, also the Argentine Republic (the last may be included as a silver country, as that nation can only procure gold at a very high premium) the currency is not in any way protected. It follows, therefore, that any of these countries would receive with wheat at

$\frac{5}{=28\cdot8}$ 26s. a quarter, nearly 29 rupees (see margin) or its equivalent in the currency of the country, whereas India with its protected currency would receive a little over 22 rupees

$\frac{2}{-=22\cdot2}$ (see margin). India is therefore handicapped to the extent of 6½ rupees per quarter of wheat. If silver fell to 15d. an ounce, and the rate of exchange with India still remained at 14d., India would still receive only 22 rupees, whereas other silver countries would be receiving 52 rupees for a quarter of $\frac{26 \times 12}{6} = 52$ wheat.

In other words, as long as the Indian mints are closed, India is crippled in her wheat trade—and unless she can produce it at a cheaper rate than other silver countries, she is practically shut out of the European market; the same remark applies to tea and other commodities.

It follows, therefore, that by keeping the Indian mints closed the prices of wheat and tea in the European markets are enhanced; if the mints were re-opened and silver remained at 27d., the price of wheat would fall to even a lower price than 26s. a quarter, as the Indian wheat trade would be thereby encouraged, and more Indian wheat would come to to the English market.

In the same way the price of Manchester cloth and coal is kept up, as will be seen by referring to Table A in Chapter II.—the higher the gold value of the rupee, the more will India be able to give in gold for these articles.

If the mints had therefore remained open, the Indian export trade would have been more flourishing, but the import trade would have contracted.

As far as trade between India and Europe is concerned, the action of the Government of India in closing the mints has had the effect of increasing the Indian import trade, and damaging the export trade to the same extent, the value of the two together being about the same as before the closing of the mints.

The real gain to India and England by

closing the mints is that the danger of India not being able to meet its gold obligations is to some extent by this action averted, and India is consequently placed in a much sounder financial position.

CHAPTER II.

THE price of silver which before the year 1873
was about 60d. an ounce troy has in the
early part of 1894 fallen to 27d.

With silver at 60d. the rupee would be
worth about two shillings; with silver at 27d.,
and the mints not closed, the value of the
rupee would be $\frac{27 \times 24}{60} = 10\frac{4}{5}$d. With the mints
closed the value of the rupee is at present
(March, 1894) about 14d.

The price of wheat in the year 1873 was
58s. a quarter; with silver at 27d., its price
should be $\frac{27 \times 58}{60} = 26\frac{1}{10}sh.$, assuming that the price
of wheat is governed by the price of silver.

There is no difficulty in showing that this must be so, as the countries producing wheat are largely countries without a gold standard, and require to be paid in the currency of the country, which is either silver or depreciated paper money. The amount that such countries have been accustomed to receive for a quarter of wheat they will still expect to receive, notwithstanding any rise or fall in the gold value of silver.

In other words, the price of wheat in a producing country with a silver currency is in no way affected by the rise or fall in the gold price of silver.

Other agricultural produce is affected by the price of wheat, and will therefore rise and fall as wheat rises and falls in price.

Many other commodities produced exclusively or principally in countries without a gold standard—such as tea, opium, indigo, hides, jute, rice, and oil seeds—will, like wheat, rise and fall with the gold price of silver.

Or what is the same thing, as gold appreciates as it becomes scarcer, more silver, wheat, tea, opium, indigo, hides, jute, rice, and oil seeds exchanges for a sovereign.

To show this clearly it will be assumed that silver is 60d. an ounce, or, what is the same thing, the rupee is worth about 24d. The price of a pound of tea in India will be assumed at 1 rupee, and that of a quarter of wheat at 20 rupees, these being exports from India. Imports into India from England, such as Manchester cloth and coal, will be assumed as selling in India at 100 rupees per bale and 5 rupees per ton respectively.

If silver fell to 45d. an ounce, the producer in India would still require only 1 rupee for a pound of tea and 20 rupees for a quarter of wheat ; he would also still be unwilling to pay more than 100 rupees for a bale of cloth, or 5 rupees for a ton of coal.

It would be still so if the gold price of silver fell to 30 or 15 pence an ounce.

The rupee in India would still purchase just as much produce of the country as before the fall in the gold price of silver. The cost of local labour will in no way have altered, and the earnings of every European and native will be precisely as it was before the fall in the gold value of silver.

The following Table A shows the price in rupees and corresponding price in gold which India could pay for cloth and coal, or would expect to receive for wheat and tea as the gold value of the rupee varied from 60 to 15 pence an ounce.

TABLE A

Price of Silver.	Value of Rupee.	Price of Wheat per Quarter.		Price of Tea per Pound.		Price of one Bale of Cloth.		Price of one Ton of Coal.	
		India.	England.	India.	England.	India.	England.	India.	England.
Pence.	Pence.	Rs.	Shs.	Rs.	Shs.	Rs.	£	Rs.	Shs.
60	24	20	40	1	2	100	10	5	10
45	18	20	30	1	1½	100	7½	5	7½
30	12	20	20	1	1	100	5	5	5
15	6	20	10	1	½	100	2½	5	2½

In all cases the cost of freight, duty, and other incidental charges are purposely omitted.

It follows, therefore, that with silver at 27d. an ounce, the rupee at 10⅘d., and wheat at 26s. a quarter, England would be offering India, the same as other silver currency countries or countries without a gold standard, viz., nearly 29 rupees a quarter of wheat, India would not be shut out of the wheat trade with Europe, as is the case at present, with the Indian mints closed. The 26 shillings offered for a quarter of wheat would represent nearly 29 rupees, instead of a little over 22. The same remark applies to all other Indian produce which that country produces in competition with other countries without a gold standard.

For the same reason India would gain in her local productions, and English trade correspondingly suffer if the mints were re-opened. English cloth and coal merchants would then only receive 10⅜d. for one rupee's worth of cloth or coal, in place of 14d., the present rate of exchange with the mints closed. If England could not supply at this price local manufactures and mines in India would be encouraged, and there would be a corresponding reduction in trade between England and India.

On the other hand India would lose in paying her gold obligations to England with the mints open. With the rupee at 14d., and these obligations taken at £18,000,000 sterling annually, the number of rupees absorbed from the revenue of India to meet this debt would be about 3,085 lacs. But 4,000 lacs of rupees would be required with the mints open, and the rupee at $10\frac{4}{5}$d., the equivalent to silver at 27d.

In this item alone India would therefore lose 4,000—3,085 = 915 lacs by the opening of the mints. If, moreover, silver fell to 15d. an ounce, this loss would be still further raised to 4,115 lacs of rupees.

India therefore loses in her export trade by the mints being closed, and the additional import trade caused thereby also affects her manufactures and mines; she, on the other hand, reaps a considerable advantage by the smaller portion of her revenue which is required to make the gold payments in England. She is also now partially protected in her currency from the effect of any further fall in the gold price of silver, and which might be so serious as to make India unable to meet her gold obligations.

CHAPTER III.

WITH THE MINTS CLOSED, SHOULD THE SECRE-TARY OF STATE FOR INDIA FIX A MINIMUM RATE FOR COUNCIL BILLS ?

To arrive at a solution of this question it is necessary to consider what makes the rate of exchange. Before the closing of the mints the price of silver undoubtedly made the rate of exchange. As long as banks and merchants had the option of buying silver for conversion into rupees, or Secretary of State drafts, the two systems of remittances competed together, and the rate of exchange depended almost entirely upon the price of silver.

With the Indian mints closed to the public the matter of exchange is placed on an entirely different footing. The banks, merchants, and the general public have now only one way of making remittances to India, and that is through the purchase of Secretary of State's drafts. The general public requiring to remit small sums buy the drafts they require from the exchange banks, but these drafts are mostly subdivided Secretary of State's drafts to meet individual requirements.

It follows therefore that, with the mints closed, the rate of exchange is entirely governed by the demand for remittance between Europe and India.

If the Secretary of State fixed a minimum rate for his Council Bills above the market rate, which in its turn depends upon the demand for bills by which remittances can be made, no tenders would be received for the bills, as naturally banks and others could not afford to pay more for the bills than the rate at which they could subsequently sell them to merchants and others.

Like all articles for sale, the price must depend upon the supply and demand. In the case of Council Bills the supply is always there, and this will continue to be the case as long as India must remit annually about £18,000,000 to England.

The price at which Council Bills can therefore be sold must depend upon the demand for bills, by which remittances can be made to India, and the same demand makes the rate of exchange.

If the demand for bills falls off, probably owing to there being a less quantity of Indian exports coming forward, the exchange banks who have a stock of bills on hand, lower the rate of exchange, in order thereby to increase the demand for bills, this in its turn tends to increase the exports from India, as merchants in England, although they may not see their way to pay say 14d. for produce of the value of one rupee, might be able to do business at 13¾d. or a fall of about two per cent.

In the same way the exchange value of the rupee rises and falls in India, but its price is regulated by the London price. If the rate falls in London, the exchange banks in India also lower the rate. This in its turn has a tendency to reduce imports into India, or, what is the same thing, to decrease the exports from England, as although a merchant in England might work at a sufficient profit if he could get 14d. for goods of the value of one rupee, he might hesitate to do business if he was only guaranteed 13¾d. for the same goods.

Through the first action of the exchange

banks the exports from India are encouraged, and through the second the exports from England are discouraged. This combined action creates a greater difference between the value of the Indian export and import trade, makes a greater demand for Council Bills, and accomplishes what the exchange banks desire.

It can therefore at once be seen that the rate of exchange cannot be fixed in an arbitrary manner, but the rate must depend upon circumstances over which the Secretary of State for India has no control.

CHAPTER IV.

THE EXPORT AND IMPORT TRADE OF INDIA, AND THEIR EFFECT ON THE CURRENCY QUESTION.

INDIA has to remit each year to England about £18,000,000 sterling; this payment must be made in gold, as England is a country with a gold standard. This payment is necessary partly for stores purchased in England, and pensions due to retired officials of the Government of India, but also for interest on loans or money borrowed in England which has been spent in covering India with a network of railways and canals and other public works of advantage to the country.

At the present rate of exchange (March, 1894), 14d. to a rupee, the Government of

India will require $\frac{18,000,000 \times 20 \times 12}{14}$ = Rs. 308,564,285,
or say 3,085 lacs of rupees. The revenues of
India are entirely raised in rupees, the currency of the country. With silver at its
present price, 27d. an ounce, the rupee, if not
protected by the closing of the mints, would
be worth $\frac{27 \times 24}{60}$ = 10$\frac{4}{5}$d., and in that case the
Government would require 4,000 lacs of rupees
to raise £18,000,000 in gold. If the exchange
value of the rupee fell to 6d., 7,200 lacs of
the Indian revenues would be required to raise
the same sum in gold. On the other hand, if
silver regained its old price of 60d. an ounce,
only 1,800 lacs of rupees would be absorbed of
the revenues of India to make its payment
of £18,000,000 to England.

If the export and import trade of India were
of equal value, the Government of India would
have to ship to England annually either 1,800

lacs, 3,085 lacs, 4,000 lacs, or 7,200 lacs of rupees, the exact sum depending upon the rate of exchange, to meet obligations due from India to England.

As a matter of fact, the annual value of the exports from India before the closing of the mints exceeded the value of the imports into India by more than £18,000,000. The Government of India was consequently under no necessity to ship rupees to England for conversion into 18,000,000 sovereigns. The exports from India being more in value than the imports by over £18,000,000 sterling, merchants in Europe required facilities to pay for this extra amount of India's produce, and which could not be covered by the imports which India absorbs from Europe. This facility is offered to. merchants and banks in Europe in the shape of Council Bills or

c

Secretary of State's drafts. Each Wednesday in the year the Secretary of State for India calls for tenders for these drafts to the amount of 30 to 60 lacs of rupees, and these bills are allotted to the highest tenderers.

In the interests of the Government of India it is therefore necessary that the value of the exports from India should continue to exceed the value of the imports annually by at least £18,000,000 sterling, or the banks and merchants in London and elsewhere would not be able to absorb the whole of the annual supply of Council Bills.

By protecting and artificially raising its gold value, as has actually been done by closing the Indian mints to the free coinage of rupees, there is some danger of the exports from India decreasing to such an extent as to make the exports only equal the imports, and in this case no part of the £18,000,000 of Council Bills could be absorbed by the banks and merchants in London and elsewhere.

By artificially raising the gold price of the rupee, the gold price of wheat, tea, and other exports are proportionately raised, as explained in Chapter II. In other countries with a silver currency like China and Mexico, the price of these exports would, however, still be based on the market price of silver, and would therefore be able to undersell India by $\frac{54 \times 100}{5 \times 14} = 77 \cdot 1$, or 22·9 per cent., taking the price of silver at 27d. an ounce and the rate of exchange with India at 14d.

It is therefore quite possible that by closing the mints in India, the exports of produce from India may be handicapped to such an extent as to damage the export trade to the annual value of £18,000,000 sterling.

In this case there would be no demand in London for Secretary of State's drafts, nor could the difficulty be met by shipping lacs of rupees to London, as the rupees would not be taken up, the value of the imports in India being sufficient to pay for the exports, and therefore banks and merchants would not require rupees.

The rupees, if sent by the Government of India to pay their gold obligations, would be of no use, as the rupee is not a current coin in the United Kingdom or anywhere else, except India ; they would therefore have to be melted up and sold at the market price of silver.

This would help to still further depress the silver market, and still more handicap India as compared to other countries with a silver currency or countries not protected by a gold standard.

This shows that any country with a silver currency that enters into gold obligations does so at great risk to its own interests, and that gold liabilities should not be incurred until something is done to fix the price of silver in relation to gold, and that until this is the case the interests of trade must suffer. It also shows how trade with India is bound up in the question of currency, and what evil effects might arise through the closing of the Indian mints.

CHAPTER V.

THE INTRODUCTION OF A GOLD STANDARD INTO THE CURRENCY OF INDIA.

IT has been explained in Chapter IV. the effect the export and import trade of India has on the currency question. It has been shown there the possible effect on India by closing the mints, and the very great difficulties that might arise owing to the export trade being destroyed to such an extent as to make it difficult for India to meet her gold liabilities.

It has been thought by many that the introduction of a gold standard into India would help the country out of her difficulties, and many methods have been proposed for introducing gold into India with a view of making a gold unit the standard of the country, and the rupee a token coin like the shilling in England.

The Government of India in June, 1893, when closing the mints to the free coinage of silver, publicly offered to give fifteen rupees for each sovereign brought to the Indian Treasuries, this being equal to a rate of exchange of 16d. to a rupee. The Indian Government appears, therefore, to have thought that its action in closing the mints would facilitate the introduction of a gold standard into the currency of India.

It can, however, easily be shown that the introduction of gold into India in such quantities as to make a gold standard in that country feasible is an utter impossibility as long as the Government of India require to remit annually £18,000,000, or any like sum, to pay its gold obligations.

If this gold obligation could by any satisfactory method be paid off, and the export and
import trade of India continue as formerly,
banks and merchants in Europe would require
to remit to India money in some manner to
pay for the excess of exports over imports.

Assuming this excess of exports over imports to remain as it was, or over £18,000,000
sterling, merchants and banks dealing with
Indian produce would require to ship to India
annually over 18 million sovereigns or its
equivalent in rupees at the exchange of the
day. As sovereigns would be more easily
obtained in Europe than rupees, which are not
easily obtained outside India, sovereigns would
therefore probably be remitted in payment.

By this means gold would be introduced into
India in large quantities, and a gold standard
could be introduced without much difficulty.

The only other method by which gold could be introduced into India in such quantities as to make a gold standard feasible would be by increasing the export trade very largely so that the annual quantity of Council Bills available would not suffice as a form of remittance to pay for the excess of exports over imports.

It has, however, been shown in Chapter IV. that, by closing the mints to the free coinage of silver, there is danger of even the present annual supply of Council Bills not being absorbed, and that as long as the mints are kept closed any increase in the export trade of India is unlikely. Therefore at present there exists no satisfactory method of introducing a gold standard into the currency of India.

CHAPTER VI.

THE SILVER PROBLEM.

THE problem as to how to restore silver to something like its old value seems no nearer solution now than it was fifteen years ago.

In 1876 the first serious fall in the price of silver took place ; but between the years 1873 and 1876 silver had a decided drooping tendency.

It was, however, in 1876 that Anglo-Indians first took serious alarm at the low rate of exchange, which for a short time fell to about 18½d. per rupee. It is useless discussing here what were the causes of the fall in the price of silver, as it is now universally acknowledged to have arisen from the following causes :

1. Appreciation of gold.
2. Depreciation of silver.
3. The restricted use of silver for purposes of currency.

Knowing, therefore, the causes for the evil, it will be endeavoured to point out a remedy.

There is, however, a further difficulty, and that is to show in a satisfactory manner that the fall in the gold price of silver is a decided evil.

There are still many who look upon this fall in silver as not an unmixed evil, and some even go so far as to say that England and other countries with a gold standard reap an advantage through the low price of silver.

It will be therefore the first object of this chapter to show that the present state of things is injurious to England, and then will be shown the remedy that should be applied.

The most important countries with a silver currency are India, China, and Mexico. To these for all practical purposes may be added the Argentine Republic and the Brazils, as neither of these countries can get gold except at a very high premium. If gold continues to appreciate in value, as seems probable, many other countries will have to be added to this list before long. It may be roughly stated that the whole world is or will be shortly divided into two hostile camps of very similar proportions, one half the world having a silver currency and the other a gold. If these two halves could live without any intercourse with each other, the present state of things might continue, and possibly the results would in no way be injurious to each other or to their respective populations.

England is, however, the greatest commer-

cial nation in the world, and must have con-
tinual intercourse with all parts of the world.
In 1846 free trade was introduced, and since
that date the commerce of the United Kingdom
has attained colossal proportions. The annual
value of her trade with the East alone amounts
to £250,000,000 sterling.

The United Kingdom depends to a great
extent upon foreign nations for its supply of
food, the sum paid away annually for this pur-
pose amounting in 1892 to £4 per head. The
total value of these imports in 1892 being
£151,000,000 sterling.

Between the years 1873 and 1892 the area
under wheat cultivation in Great Britain has
fallen from 11·2 to 5·8 per cent., or about one-
half the area under wheat in 1873 has since
gone out of wheat cultivation. Much of the
land in Wiltshire, Essex, and other parts is at

present unsaleable at any price, and agriculture is in such a depressed state that with any further fall in the price of agricultural produce it would seem impossible for agriculture to continue to exist in Great Britain as an industry.

This state of things has been partly brought about by the people of Great Britain themselves. England has assisted with her riches to develop countries with a silver currency. Great Britain has advanced many millions sterling to the Argentine Republic, Brazils, Mexico, India, and China, to assist these countries in constructing railways, harbours, canals, and other public works of utility. By means of English capital these countries are now able to supply England with the foreign food she requires, and at prices with which she herself is at present unable to compete.

Wheat between 1873 and 1894 has fallen from 58s. to 26s. a quarter, barley from 40s. to 25s., and other agricultural produce in proportion.

It has been shown in Chapters I. and II. how the gold price of silver affects the price of agricultural produce in Great Britain. It has also been shown in Chapter II. how the fall in the gold price of silver has brought India to the verge of bankruptcy. What applies to India applies even more to other countries with a silver currency. Guatemela has lately stated through her Government her inability to continue to pay her gold obligations owing to the depreciation in the gold price of silver. Mexico is in much the same plight, and unless there is some recovery in the gold price of silver it will be difficult for that country to continue to meet its gold obligations. Other South American nations are not able to pay the interest on their foreign debt, partly owing to the appreciation of gold. Some of the European States are bankrupt or on the eve of bankruptcy, owing partly to the low price of produce caused by the fall in the gold value of silver. Most of the European States whose people have to depend upon agricultural produce for their livelihood, even more than the people of Great Britain, are suffering in the same way from the low price of produce. In some States protective duties have been introduced with a view of raising the price of native produce, but although this duty may enhance the price locally of the particular produce upon which it is placed, little if any good can result to that nation, as protective duties injure trade as a whole, as it tends to lower the imports, and in this case the exports must also suffer.

There is also another aspect of the question which has become serious to the United Kingdom and other nations with a gold standard. The actual value of silver in the shillings at the present time is only about $\frac{27 \times 12}{60} = 5\frac{2}{3}$d., the actual value of silver in a five-franc piece is $\frac{27 \times 500}{60} = 225$ centimes. This gives an immense inducement to illicit coinage.

It is true that in England only forty shillings of silver is legal tender, but this is little protection, as it is extremely easy to pay one's way with silver in England. A few enterprising men, or even a native State in India, or perhaps a small South American Republic, could easily obtain the necessary appliances, and, without much fear of discovery, manufacture shillings, half-crowns, francs, and five-franc pieces by the ton, and thereby making a profit of over 100 per cent. No conscientious scruple

D

need restrict such manufacture, as the coins manufactured would be what they were represented to be—viz., silver. Who can say that this practice may not now be in extensive operation ?

It is possible the present price of silver, 27d., may restrict the outturn to such an extent as to make some recovery possible, but the same was said when silver was at a much higher price. On the other hand, silver might fall to 15d. This cannot be regarded as an impossibility.

When silver was at 60d. its fall to 27d. would have been ridiculed by all. It has, however, now fallen to this figure.

The Broken Hill Mine in Australia sends weekly 250,000 ounces of silver to the market, and can produce it at 22½d. per ounce. Other mines with improved machinery may be able to produce it at a lower price, and even the Australian mine might find it possible by greater economy to produce it at a lower figure.

Enough has now been said to show the injurious effects on the United Kingdom and other countries of the great fall in the gold value of silver, and the author will now point out the remedy that he thinks should be applied.

The principal remedy advocated to raise the gold price of silver is international bimetallism. It is thought by many that the different countries interested in the question could settle by international agreement (the same as the Postal Union settle an universal price for letter postage) a fixed ratio at which the Governments concerned would agree to accept silver equally with gold in payment for all taxes, duties, and other revenue purposes.

Until the year 1873 several of the countries
of Europe did accept either silver or gold at a
ratio of 15½ of silver to 1 of gold.   Up to this
date the price of silver kept steady at about 6od.
an ounce, and the bimetallists argue that it
was owing to this practice on the part of these
countries that the price of silver did not fluc-
tuate much before 1873.   They go further and
say that if the remaining countries of Europe
had agreed to accept silver payments equally
with gold at the same ratio, the silver problem
would never have been heard of.   However
that may be, the bimetallists are undoubtedly
right in dating the disastrous fall in the price of
silver from the year 1873.   It must, however,
be borne in mind that the outturn of silver has
immensely increased since 1873 as compared
to gold, and it would seem that those nations
who possessed a gold standard and a token

silver coinage at that time were quite justified in their own interests in adhering to this standard. At that time any departure from the gold standard would have been strongly resisted in England, and bimetallism could therefore not have been introduced.

It is, however, useless, discussing further what might have been done in 1873—the problem is what should be done for the good of the world, and Great Britain and India in particular, in the year 1894.

International bimetallism, although still possible, could only be introduced with great difficulty, as the consent and agreement of so many nations would be necessary. Some system of raising the price of silver to which a less number of nations would require to give their consent and adherence seems more feasible.

The principal silver mines are situated in the United States, Mexico, and Australia.

Whatever arrangement is made must therefore at first be made with these three countries.

The outturn from the mines in the United States is over 50,000,000 ounces per annum, and the balance comes principally from Australia and Mexico.

These three nations would be naturally interested in any scheme for raising the gold value of silver, as they would then be able to purchase the same amount of gold with a less quantity of silver. It would not, however, be just to nations outside those producing silver to take any special action as regards silver without doing the same as regards gold.

Both precious metals should be treated in the same manner and have the same advantages. They are both used principally for

currency purposes, and therefore require special treatment and protection. Although at
the present time gold is appreciating in value
because of its scarcity, and silver depreciating
because of its quantity, the reverse may happen
at any time, and therefore what is now done
should not deal only with the present state of
things, but with what might be the state of
things at some future day.

The principal gold-producing countries are
also silver-producing ; the only other States
largely interested in the question, and who
would probably also have to be consulted,
would be the States of South Africa.

Great Britain as one of the nations, and perhaps the nation most interested in the question,
should through its Government take up the
question in a practical manner.   It should
invite the nations interested largely in the pro-

duction of gold and silver to send representatives to a conference to be held in London. At this conference Great Britain should be represented in the interest of her colonies in Australia and South Africa, and an effort should be made at this conference to come to an agreement on the following points :—

1. Gold and silver to be in future a monopoly of the Government in whose territory the mines are situated, the same as opium is a monopoly of the Government of India.

2. All gold and silver produced and not required for coinage in the country where it is mined to be shipped to London and sold at a rate to be fixed by the conference.

3. The conference to meet periodically, as may be agreed.

There would probably be no difficulty in the conference coming to an effective agreement on these points, and the details of the arrangement could be subsequently easily arranged. All the countries represented at the conference would be only too eager to have the question settled in such a manner as to make the great depression in trade caused by the appreciation of gold and depreciation in silver that has occurred in recent years an impossibility in the future.

CHAPTER VII.

SHOULD THE INDIAN MINTS BE RE-OPENED TO FREE COINAGE?

IT HAS been shown in previous chapters in what manner the closing of the Indian mints has affected trade, both in India and England. In India the export trade has suffered, and manufactures and mines are placed at a certain disadvantage in competition with England and also China.

In England the export trade to India has been encouraged by the action of closing the Indian mints, and the price of wheat and other produce of India is kept up in England at a higher price than would be the case if the mints were re-opened and the rupee dropped to its natural price of 10⅜d. with silver at 27d. an ounce.

Manufacturers and farmers in England have therefore gained by the closing of the mints, but India has suffered both in her exports and manufactures.

India has, however, reaped an advantage for the time by the smaller number of rupees that are absorbed from her revenues in order to pay her gold debt to England.

It has been shown that by re-opening the mints there is a possibility that India would in this case not be able to meet her gold obligations in England. Even now with the mints closed, a deficit is anticipated in the Indian revenues for the financial year 1894-95 of Rs. 29,230,000, and import duties have been imposed to partly meet this deficit.

On the other hand, it is possible that if the

mints remain closed the export trade of India will suffer to such an extent as to make little or no demand for Council Bills, and if this were to happen India, in this case, would also find it difficult to meet her gold obligations.

With the mints closed or open there is therefore some danger of India's bankruptcy, but the financial state of India is made safer by the closing of the mints.

There is also no way at present of introducing gold into India in such quantities as to make a gold standard feasible.

Nearly the whole difficulty of the situation is caused by the gold obligations due from India to England. If these could be got out of the way, and the exports from India restored to what they were previous to the closing of the mints, gold would go to India, as Council Bills would not be available.

Every effort should therefore be made by the Government of India to reduce the annual sum to be remitted to England. The conversion of the gold debt into a rupee debt appears an impossibility, as the principal gold loans cannot be paid off until the years 1931 and 1948. There is, however, a large annual amount of gold payments due from India to England for railway material and other stores. In these days of severe competition there would be no difficulty in getting firms who tender to deliver stores to make their tenders in rupees, and to take payment on delivery in India. Firms in India should also be encouraged to submit tenders for the same stores. In this manner some reduction in India's gold payments would be made, and the manufacture of railway material and other stores in India encouraged.

All future engagements of Indian officials

should be based on payments in the currency of the country, and the same remark should apply to all pensions and furlough allowances. No further loans should be raised in gold, but any additional funds required by the Government of India for the construction of railways or other purposes should be raised in India in the currency of the country.

If these suggestions are carried out, a considerable reduction in the gold payments due from India to England would be certain, the consequence would be that there would be a less quantity of Council Bills on the London market, and therefore a better price obtained for them.

At the present time (March, 1894) when there is a comparative large number of Council Bills required to pay for the exports coming forward from India, exchange rules under 14d., or about 3d. above the value of the silver in the rupee. When silver was 32d. an ounce, the rupee stood at about 15d., or about 2d. above the value of silver in the rupee. If silver does not rise much above its present price of 27d. an ounce, the rupee will probably fall to under 13d., when the Indian export season is over. The effect of closing the mints is therefore to keep the price of the rupee 2d. to 3d. above its natural value. ; and if the whole of the annual supply of Council Bills can be disposed of whilst exchange is kept up about 20 per cent., it would seem best to keep the mints closed.

Until the gold obligations due from India to England are very considerably reduced, it will be impossible to do much more to assist the currency of India.

If India and Great Britain stood alone, the

last being compelled to purchase the produce of the first, nothing further would require to be attempted. As the Council Bills became less in quantity they would rise in price, and if the Indian export trade could be encouraged at the same time as exchange rose, India would soon be out of her currency difficulty.

There are, however, other silver currency countries who produce what India produces, and therefore the higher exchange rises, owing to the closing of the mints, the less is her export trade, this trade being transferred to other silver currency countries where the currency is in no way protected.

Until international Bimetallism is introduced or gold and silver protection, as described in Chapter VI., it is useless looking forward to any great expansion in the export trade of India.

When, however, some agreement has been come to regarding the relative price of the precious metals, all silver currency countries will be on the same footing, and the Indian mints should then be re-opened to free coinage. India with her cheap labour and other advantages will be then certain to rapidly increase her export trade. If in the meantime the annual supply of Secretary of State's drafts in London have been very considerably reduced, gold will be certain to flow to India, and the Indian Government will be able to introduce a gold standard if thought desirable.

When these results have been accomplished the currency of India, after passing through severe vicissitudes. will be at last placed on a secure footing.

EXPLANATORY NOTES.

One lac = 100,000 rupees.

One crore = 10,000,000 rupees.

Fractions in the foregoing pages are, as much as possible, omitted for the sake of simplicity.

The value of silver in the rupee and two-shilling piece is taken as equal, although actually the rupee has 180 grains of silver and the florin 174·54 grains.

The price of standard silver with the rupee at par or two shillings is taken at 60 pence per ounce troy.